IN THE BEGINNING
THERE WAS
GOD, ME
& You

THE TRUE LOVE STORY THAT ONLY GOD COULD HAVE WRITTEN

Angie BEE & Bartee

Reading for the Whole Person

INSPIRED published by

Ladero Press LLC

229 Kettering Road

Deltona, Florida 32725

First Ladero Press Printing, July 2017

Second Ladero Press Printing, April 2021

In the Beginning: There Was God, Me & You

Copyright © 2017 by Angela Neal and Eugene Neal

Contributions from members of *The TOUR that Angie BEE Presents*

All rights reserved.

ISBN: 978-1-946981-05-9 Paperback / 978-1-946981-06-6 EPUB 978-1-946981-07-3 MOBI

Printed in the United States of America

Set in Quattrocento Sans and Cinzel Regular

Cover Designed by SheerGenius

Edited by Spirit of Excellence Writing & Editing Services, LLC

Front Cover Photo Credit: J. Simmons

Back Cover Photo Credit: Jhonn De La Puente

Scripture quotations are taken from the Holy Bible, New Living Translation, Copyright ©1996, 2004, 2007, 2013, 2015 by Tyndale House Foundation. Used by permission of Tyndale House Publishers, Inc., Carol Stream, Illinois 60188. All rights reserved.

All rights reserved. The reproduction, transmission, or utilization of this work in whole or in part in any form by any electronic, mechanical or other means, now known or hereafter invented, including xerography, photocopying and recording, or in any information storage or retrieval system, is forbidden without written permission. For permission, please contact *Ladero Press Editors at* editors@laderopress.com.

The INSPIRED logo is a trademark of Ladero Press.

The *Where Writers Can Soar* logo is a trademark of Ladero Press.

Library of Congress information available upon request.

www.laderopress.com

www.DaQueenBee.com

Table of Contents

Foreword 5

Acknowledgements 7

In the Beginning 11

Bartee 14

"Da Queen Bee" Angie BEE 18

Their Courthouse Wedding 22

Thank You for Your Patience 29

Is That His First Name? 32

The Music in Me 35

After the Deaths, He Enlarged Our Territory 45

Blessings 48

Transitions 50

Now, Back to the Love! 52

Back at the Courthouse 58

She Was There! 60

A Word from God 65

Foreword

I was honored by the Lord to witness the official union of this beautiful couple as Bartee proposed at Angie BEE's birthday dinner on May 8, 2013. From that moment on, I could not even remember what her life was like before him, especially regarding ministry and business. I love to see them together because they look as though they've been married for twenty years, yet they're still in the honeymoon phase. I can't help but smile every time I see a photo of them together - they're always smiling.

The first time that I visited their home in Daytona, I was in tears because I saw the Bible so clearly manifested in their relationship. They are truly a blended family, and I have never heard them say "hers" or "his" -- everything is about "ours" -- from their children to their Kingdom assignments. By being in their presence, I have learned so much about real love and the purpose of covenant marriage. Through the testimony that they share in this book, you will be able to see how the Holy Spirit can strategically lead and guide you to the Father's perfect will. Be prepared to laugh, cry, and glean valuable insight about divine connections.

Sharlyne C. Thomas, Founder
Sword of the Spirit Ministries Florida, Inc.

www.TakeUpThySword.com

Acknowledgements

Angie BEE & Bartee want to first give God all the honor and praise, not only for our union, but for His direction in our lives. Without Him, our love would not be possible, and this book would never have been written.

We thank our children: Angelyn, Eugene, Jasmine, and Edward. You each had to acknowledge our relationship and union, and we thank you for accepting us in your own ways.

Thanks to the members of *The TOUR that Angie BEE Presents* for caring for us, covering us, working with us, and allowing us to minister side-by-side. Thanks especially to Tahara Thompson, Sharlyne C. Thomas, Gwendolyn Thomas (no relation), the rest of the ministry members, friends, and family that were there with us ... from the beginning.

IN THE BEGINNING
THERE WAS
GOD, ME
& You

In the Beginning

―― ∾ ――

"Dearly Beloved, we are gathered together to get through this thing called LIFE." These are the lyrics of a song entitled "Let's Go Crazy", which was written by Prince and is known around the world. It also is the opening line for many marriage ceremonies. I remember when I was asked to officiate my first wedding; I was SO SCARED that I would accidentally sound like Prince when I delivered that opening line!

In the beginning God created the heavens and the earth.

This is the very first verse in the New Living Translation of the Holy Bible, Genesis 1:1. If you get caught up reading the rest of that chapter, you will soon find the following in Genesis 1:27.

So God created human beings[d] in his own image. In the image of God he created them; male and female he created them.

Dearly beloved, in the beginning, God created male and female. *In the Beginning: There was God, Me & You.* Thank you, Father!

This book is a true love story about how Bartee met Angie BEE (that's me), and together we glorify God in our home, through our businesses, and by sharing the gospel of Jesus Christ. Did we start a church? No. We simply "are" the church, and we reach other children of God and demonstrate His love through our actions. Is our marriage perfect? No. We aren't perfect people, but by sharing our story with others, we give inspiration and praise to our Father (Psalm 111:1, NLT). This book is a true love story - and it is YOUR love story, too; because in the beginning, God was with YOU!

Due to my disability, I didn't have a job but I DID volunteer at an Orlando-based, gospel radio station. The owner of the station was a jovial young man named Jarvis who LOVED the LORD, LOVED his WIFE, and LOVED his CHILDREN ... in that order! Yes, Lord! Jarvis played the organ, and every pastor in town wanted him to play at their churches on Sunday morning. He even had a nickname: "B3 Hammond Prophet." Sometimes, when I would get to the station, he would be rehearsing a song on his keyboard, and the whole radio station sounded like church.

YES, LORD! I loved being at the radio station. My radio show debuted in 2008 on the Jericho Broadcast Network as the nation's first holy hip-hop music format show airing weekdays in a time slot. My show was on the air four hours a day. I played music, interviewed rappers and tried to tell my version of what I had learned from church and bible study the week before. Listeners were global as the show was streamed on the Internet; and now, Jarvis had invited me to air my show on his local station from 8 PM to midnight. It was a blast! Folks were in and out of the station all day; there was a soul food restaurant across the hall (YUM!); and Jarvis was planning his one-year anniversary of the radio station in that location. "Jarvis, let me bring the rappers in during the anniversary to broadcast live on the air," I asked him.

"Sure!" he beamed... and then, it was so.

Bartee

Bartee was a man with a plan: go to work, get off work, and have as much fun as a man could legally have. His career with the County discouraged him from getting into TOO much trouble, because testing positive for drugs or alcohol could find him in the unemployment line; so, he had fun in other ways. After all, he had been divorced for a few years now, and since he lived only a few minutes' drive from his sons, they were content on seeing him daily, so Bartee was free to burn through a weekend!

His ritual began on Thursday night when he would apply shaving cream to his face and bald head. He decided some years earlier to become "bald by choice" after seeing bald Michael Jordan wearing an earring. Bartee said, "I looked at the TV screen and saw Michael with that bald head and earring, and I thought to myself, 'I would look good with an earring!'." So, the ritual began.

He would carefully apply the cream and sit in front of the TV for about two hours, enjoying action movies and any sporting event that was on TV that season. He lived in a rented three-bedroom house on a lake and did his own landscaping and interior decorating, so artistically sculpturing his beard with shaving cream was a delicate process that could not be rushed! After about two hours (maybe three if he fell asleep on the couch), he would rise, shower, clean his kitchen, and get ready for the weekend!

Bartee's official weekend began every Friday at 5:01 PM when his shift at the courthouse ended. He has spent a couple of decades working for the Florida court system in Volusia County (more specifically, in the DeLand Courthouse). I remember the first time I went to visit him at the courthouse and my GPS directed me to drive by Stetson University! What a lovely campus! What a nice courthouse! I mean, if you are visiting the courthouse to see your hubby, it can be a nice place to visit; otherwise, that place may not make you smile … but I am getting ahead of the story.

When Bartee got off work, it was like the last day of school before summer vacation… peeling his car out of the parking garage, making the 45-minute commute back home to change out of his uniform and get in to his "play" clothes. If Bartee's buddies were doing something, he was with them. If they WEREN'T doing something, he was calling to say to them, "Where YOU at?" If he got off work in DeLand at 5 PM on a Friday night, he could be home by 5:30 PM, showered and redressed by 6 PM, and out the door before 7 PM. His goal was to cram in as much fun as he could before heading back to the courthouse on Monday morning at 8 AM.

Bartee is an R&B singer who, by his own admission, is stuck in the 70s. His smooth jazz, R&B and vintage soul repertoire of songs keep him booked for corporate engagements, civic, and even private performances. Bartee can make a Motown song sound like it should have been written <u>that</u> way in the first place, and the women LOVE to hear him sing! My great-grandmother (affectionately referred to as Big Mama) used to say, "You know you doing something right when the White AND the Colored want to be around you" – that describes Bartee's performances. In lieu of a band, he sings to instrumental tracks; and in lieu of a DJ, he brings and operates his own equipment. This one-man-band doesn't seem to bother the women as they encourage him to dance with them during each song and in between the songs, too! I'm pretty sure that there were plenty of tips and phone numbers placed in his hands over the years, but I will let him tell you that part of the story when he is ready. If Bartee wasn't singing on a Friday night, he was singing on a Saturday night, AND EVERYBODY from DeLand to Daytona to Ormond Beach and Port Orange had heard about him.

"Da Queen Bee" Angie BEE

Now, on the other hand, there was me, Angie BEE. I was hanging with a gang of Christian rappers a few years ago, traveling to bring Friday night rap concerts and Saturday morning workshops. I am the leader of *The TOUR that Angie BEE Presents*, an evangelism troupe founded in July 2011. I wrote my first book in 2011, so, between sharing my testimony, selling books, and scheduling *The TOUR* to bring our concerts ... my weekends were a bit different from Bartee's.

My first husband had left me when our two daughters were toddlers. My second husband was abusive to me and my daughters, and I was learning to manage my medicated symptoms from major depression and anxiety ... so I was not thinking about a man! All they do is love you, hurt you, leave you, and disease you; so, I was finished. The only man for me was GOD, and I was hearing His voice clearly in my head and doing my best to follow His directions. I was taking Psalm 100:2 to heart in that I was *serving the Lord with gladness*. I couldn't sing (at least my daddy told me that I couldn't), so I would just rap along at the concerts and ignore the fact that I couldn't hold a tune. Each of the rappers knew that I loved them as only a mother could love a God-child, and I had memorized all their songs…so, I was enjoying my life and rapping His praises.

Now, I had a weekend ritual as well. On Monday, I was asking the Lord what He wanted me to wear to the concert that I was scheduled to MC on Friday night. By Wednesday, the Lord would send some money my way, and by Thursday, I would have found the PERFECT gown with the money that God had sent me. I say that He sent me money because I was declared disabled in 2010. The monthly check that I got on the third of each month was less than $900.00, and I had an apartment, a car note, and I needed to eat regularly and drive to the outreach concerts. The food stamps (EBT card) helped with the food; but most times, our concerts were more than fifty miles from my home, and I needed to be sure I could get to the destination and return. Well, I THOUGHT I needed to be sure of this, but God had it all worked out.

Generally, a few days before each concert, someone would put some money in my hands to "bless me", or they would buy some extra books that I know they didn't need. Sometimes, a person would ask me to create a flyer for them even though I ain't no graphic designer, or they would send me a love offering because my book touched them. It never failed – God ALWAYS provided. Whatever money would come in would be JUST ENOUGH to get me a new dress or shoes or hair or nails; fill up the tank to get us to the concert; and sometimes, even buy my dinner after the concert ended. The food stamps helped me get snacks for the car ride, and the host always covered our hotel room. We saw kids come to Christ; we had parents praising and testifying; and God was glorified in all that we went through. On Sunday mornings and Wednesday evenings, I was in a church building somewhere learning the Word of God, and I beamed with honor to be used by Him.

One day, God told me to gather two mothers. The three of us would share our testimonies in a workshop setting. He showed me the logo design and the format. He told me not to plan the program – just plan the location and the date, and then invite the mothers; He would do the rest.

In January 2013, the first *Moms-n-Ministry* workshop took place, and God was faithful in His participation. I had no script, no format structure, no plan. The vendors arrived before I did, and I didn't even know what my speakers were going to say. My pastor at the time operated the sound system; the first lady gleefully hosted; and I watched *The TOUR* grow before my eyes. I later realized that the date of that workshop was the anniversary date of when the devil first tried to kill me. In January 1995, my daughters and I had been hit head-on by an 18-wheel semi-tractor trailer truck, and we all lived to tell others about it. Thank you, Lord.

Fast-forward to August of that same year. I had married, moved to Daytona Beach from Orlando, and was leading an outreach ministry that included concerts, three workshops, a music mix-tape, and our own in-house DJ. The gift of prophecy had been planted in me, so I was preaching, prophesying, and speaking at events with my husband by my side for it all.

That was the beginning. Now, let US tell you the REST of the story.

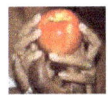

Their Courthouse Wedding

"Dearly Beloved, we are gathered together to get through this thing called LIFE." I just KNEW the court officer was going to say those words as she stepped to the front of this little chapel to marry my friends. One of my newest Christian rappers, JR Bartee (not to be confused with MY Bartee, but I'll explain the initials later), was getting married to his girlfriend (his daughter's mother), and I was SO excited for them both!

When I first met JR and his family in November 2012, I asked him if he was going to marry her; and three months later, there was genuine growth between the two! During that time, they had moved to my city and joined the church where I was a member. Our pastor had encouraged them, and the entire congregation even attended a marriage workshop in February 2013. At the end of the weeklong workshop, JR proposed to his girlfriend; and about a week later, they found themselves at the DeLand courthouse wedding chapel!

On the morning of their wedding in mid-February, I didn't feel like getting up much less getting dressed. The anxiety symptoms had been kicking my behind, and I was more tired than usual. Another rapper from *The TOUR* and his pregnant wife had been staying with me in my one-bedroom apartment; and although they were certainly welcome in my home, I think I was missing my bed. I had another friend camping out on an air mattress in what should have been the dining room, and I was sleeping on my couch. My daughters and I had spent time being homeless and living in Extended Stay hotels years earlier, so I wasn't about to have nobody that I call a friend having to go that route!

We were all just chilling at the apartment when JR called to say that he and his fiancée were headed to the courthouse. WHAT?! Look at God! Now, I *gotta* throw on some "Queen Bee" clothes and head out the door with my camera. Oh, well! No complaining when God is orchestrating; let's go!

We drove the forty-five minutes or so from my apartment home in Winter Park to the VERY SAME COURTHOUSE in DeLand where Bartee works. *Do you see what God was doing there?!* I arrived just in time to see JR in his suit, beaming with pride. We were gathered in the courtyard taking pictures, congratulating him, and then, I spotted his infant daughter. Such a cutie she was, sitting in her baby carrier! I started focusing my camera lens to snap a picture of her when all of a sudden, this big, round, bald head dips right in my shot! *Who is this old man, and can't he see that I'm taking a picture?!*

The short, little man then proceeded to play with the baby and coo all over her. I watched him walk over to all of JR's family as they gathered in the courtyard; and he hugged and greeted and loved on each of them like he was the family patriarch or something. "Who IS that man?" I asked the soon-to-be groom. I knew that JR's dad had gone to heaven decades before, and I had met his mom at an earlier concert, so I was just being nosy.

"That's my uncle," JR replied. "His name is Bartee, too!"

Uncle Bartee – that's what I called him. This short, little, round, bald, chocolate man was my rapper's uncle, and the hand of God was ALL over him.

The family gathered in the chapel, and the ceremony began. Our pastor at the time arrived with our first lady, and we all began to snap pictures and videotape. There were smiles and hugs and love, and then Uncle Bartee stepped forward to sign the marriage certificate as a witness. We all walked outside to leave the courthouse and I looked around for Uncle Bartee.

"He's got to head back to work, Auntie," JR told me. "He took his lunch break to be with us."

Now, when JR first became a member of *The TOUR*, he immediately began calling me "Auntie Angie", and he remained the only rapper to do so. I don't really remember why he called me that … everybody else called me "Da Queen Bee", and one rapper even called me "Ma", but nobody else called me "Auntie."

We all headed home, and when I got in front of my computer, I started to review the pictures we snapped. Such a beautiful family and such a sweet ceremony! I remembered praying and thanking the Lord for that day, but somewhere in my mind, Uncle Bartee kept popping up.

"Give my number to your uncle and tell him to give me a call," I asked JR one evening when we were in the recording studio at church. Uncle Bartee had come to my mind, and I wondered what he was doing and why he hadn't come out to more of our local concerts.

JR had shared with me how this man had been a surrogate father to him after his dad died. Uncle Bartee would pick up his nephew and take him to family reunions and outings, just like he was one of his own sons. Now that JR was out evangelizing through his songs and sharing his testimony, I wondered where his uncle was.

"Unc don't do church, Auntie Angie. He do his own thang. You don't want to talk to him – he sings R&B music!" he explained.

"I didn't ask you what kind of music he sang, Nephew! Just do what I asked you to do!" I scolded. (The Christian rappers on *The TOUR* with me must think that I don't listen to Country music or R&B or Jazz music or ANYTHING ELSE! LOL).

Sometimes, I really did feel like I was some grown man's mama ... although God had given me two daughters. Ministry on the road is a blessing, but sometimes the folks that accompany you can be demanding with their questioning and lack of preparation. I guess it didn't help that I was the only woman on *The TOUR*, and it seemed like all the rappers acted like I was their manager or mother or something.

> *"Angie BEE, where are we gonna eat after the concert?"*
> *"Angie BEE, I need you to introduce me like this!"*
> *"Angie BEE, can I ride to the concert with you?"*
> *"Angie BEE, give me directions to the concert"*
> *"Angie BEE...!!!!!!"*

Now, JR was asking me why I wanted his uncle to call me. *Hmmph?* I didn't even know the answer to that question; I was just following the lead that was in my head, and my defensive side didn't feel like I owed JR an explanation to my head.

Why DID I want Uncle Bartee to call me? He wasn't my type, and I wasn't gonna be bothered with no man ever again! He was short; I like tall men. His belly was round; mine was, too, so that wasn't gonna work. He had stepped in front of my camera angle and didn't even say "excuse me", so he must be rude. Actually, when JR introduced us at his wedding, Uncle Bartee just shook my hand and kept it moving! Now, I am a FINE woman and NO MAN HAS EVER kept it moving after seeing me! Even when I was two hundred pounds heavier, I was still turning heads, and this man ain't even SMILE at me?

Hmmph. Uncle Bartee must be another blind R&B singer.

No worries ... I'm serving the Lord with gladness, and HE alone supplies all my needs. Besides, I ain't interested in no man! All they do is leave you, hurt you, abandon you, abuse you, rape you, smack you, steal from you, and dishonor you. I've got a man in my life in heaven and on earth. Never mind him anyway ...

It's the last week in February, so it's time for my annual vacation visit with MY [earthly] DADDY!!

Thank You for Your Patience

Every year, my parents make their yearly drive from Detroit to Kissimmee, Florida, where they own a timeshare. For that week, I lose myself in sitting, talking, and just BEING with my family. My kids are grown and doing their own thing, so this week is special to me because it is ME time with my dad and stepmom. The day after they checked in, I was driving to the timeshare with my suitcase in my car when the phone rang.

"Hello, this is Bartee."

"Hey, Uncle Bartee! How ya doing?" I gleefully replied.

This was the first time HE had initiated a phone call to me since his nephew's wedding a couple of weeks earlier. Since obtaining his phone number from JR, I had called him once or twice before to thank him for supporting his nephew and to learn more about him, but the TV would be so loud in his home, and his baritone voice mumbled so badly, the conversation never lasted past five minutes. In fact, it seemed as if this man shaved every night before going to bed because he would inevitably say to me, "I can't talk now; I got this shave stuff on my face", and that phone call would be over. I had come to the conclusion that he didn't want to hold a conversation with me, and it had been a while since I had called him, but now he was calling me! Was there something wrong?

His voice was clear and mumble-free during this conversation, and I promptly answered each question he presented to me until I realized that he was trying to ask me out on a date. WHAT?! NOW?! TONIGHT?! Oh, Lord, no ... this man's timing WAS off because I'm going to see my daddy now!

"Listen, Bartee, I would love to go on a date with you, but my daddy is in town, and I am headed to see him for a week. I will be back in Orlando next weekend. May I have a rain check?"

His voice sounded a bit deflated as he replied that he would call me again next week. I promptly said to him, "Thank you for your patience."

By the time I arrived at the timeshare, my daddy could have been the first man on the moon, but I was no more interested in hanging out there. I think my stepmom noticed something was different because I kept going outside to use my cell phone. There is no cell phone service in the timeshare, so you have to go outside to get a signal. I must have called Bartee a dozen times during that week, and each time I called him ... his voice seemed to get a bit clearer.

Is That His First Name?

"Angie BEE, this is Bartee," the voice on the other end of the phone said to me.

Our rapper Bartee was the only member of *The TOUR* that called me "Auntie", and I knew this voice on my phone wasn't my "nephew's" voice, so it must have been that round, bald, blind man.

"Uncle Bartee?" I asked.

"Yes," he replied, "JR is my nephew."

Until that moment, I never knew JR's first name! We always called him "Bartee." In the Christian rap community, we ALL have stage names and names that God gave us, so I sometimes don't remember "real" names. You should hear me on the phone trying to book our travel arrangements: "Well, I need a room for *C-Dub*, *Determined* and *Fava*; *Kilo* and *BossMan* need rooms and so do ..." (you get the picture). Now, Mr. Short-ness was calling my nephew by his first name ... or initials ... or ... (you get the point).

"Yes, Uncle Bartee! It is a pleasure to hear your voice again! Your nephew talks a lot about you," I said.

"Well," he continued, "JR invited me to a radio station tonight, and I'm calling you to get directions."

"Directions to the studio in Orlando? Don't you live in Daytona Beach?" I asked.

"Yeah, I do. What are the directions to get to Orlando from where I am?"

This man is driving over an hour to see his nephew? WOW! Such wonderful support! That is so special!

"I'll give you the address so you can program your GPS."

"Just tell me how to get there, and I will write it down," he replied. My heart just melted as I heard him crumple some paper and attempt to scratch the directions down with an empty ink pen. "Hold on a minute; this pen ain't working," he said.

"Would you like me to text you the address?" I asked.

"Naw, I don't text," he replied.

WHAT?!!? No text? No GPS? He must be calling me from a rotary phone. He must REALLY be old!

"Okay, I'm ready," he said, returning to the phone. I gave him the address, landmarks, and directions; I told him that I looked forward to seeing him at the radio station later on.

That was a Friday night.

The Music in Me

"Who is that gentleman sitting in the corner over there, Angie BEE?" Jarvis asked me as I buzzed around the radio station.

The open house was filled with guests, all trying to give a shout out on the air. There were callers and folks Skyping in; I was chatting on the webcam with international listeners on oOvoO.com and via Facebook. The rappers from *The TOUR that Angie BEE Presents* were having a ball, and Mama Rita was even in the house. Mama Rita leads an outreach ministry that takes Christian rappers to minister in juvenile detention centers, so we were a perfect, partnering match. She booked the jails, and I brought the crew. She was a bit outspoken (to say the least), and I didn't mind pulling the reins on her mouth, as only a spiritual daughter could do. This sixty-year-old white woman LOVED HER some Christian rap music and was fond of black men, as she had multiracial children and grandchildren, too. She was the loudest thing in the studio at that moment.

"I don't know who you talking 'bout, Jarvis ... What gentleman?" I replied. As Jarvis nodded his head in the direction where my eyes followed, Mama Rita caught my glance.

"I would take Pops with me on the road, Angie BEE, but he looks too slow to keep up with me!" she proclaimed loudly. She then proceeded to dance to the music and munch on refreshments.

I then realized that Uncle Bartee was sitting in the corner all by himself. He seemed to be half asleep but truly interested in what was going on around him. He almost seemed a bit lonely, but I couldn't dwell on him at that moment. The webcam was chiming, and I needed to introduce the next rapper who was scheduled to "spit on the mic" – LIVE! Freestyle was my favorite aspect of this ministry, and JR was about to hit the microphone with his uncle in the studio. I kept on working ... Uncle Bartee kept on sitting. The music kept on praising, and God kept on putting His plan in action.

"I think I see something going on in the Spirit here, Angie BEE," beamed Jarvis.

"Whatcha talking about, Boss?" I inquired.

"I just feel something growing in the atmosphere around here, and it's all around you," he replied. "Pretty sure it has something to do with that boy's uncle," he continued.

"WHAT?!" That man don't even see me!" I proclaimed. "He ain't interested, and I am too busy buzzin'!"

"We'll see!" Jarvis replied.

His smile was big and deep, and there was something in his eye that let me know that he was serious. After all, Jarvis was very well- known as the best Hammond Organist in the city, and the prophetic call on his life was a blessing to be around. So, who was I to question this inquiry from the "Hammond B3 Prophet"?

(from left to right)
Recording artist "Determined", "Uncle Bartee" and JR Bartee

Now, let me rewind the story just a bit. A couple of months earlier, my pastor at the time had called a meeting to inform us leaders that we were having an auto show in the mall parking lot. The church was in the same strip mall with a large grocery story, so parking was plentiful. During my servitude season, I sat on the founding Board of Directors of one church in Orlando, and now, I was the Promotions Director and Evangelism Board Member of my new church home. All I needed to do was book the rappers to do a concert during the auto show and MC. Maybe, I could also announce the event during my radio show ... and maybe ask Jarvis to sponsor the show and ... *you get the point*.

The plans were to hold the church auto show on the Saturday morning AFTER the open house at the radio station where the rappers were to be featured on air.

Of course, with this added date to the schedule, this meant a full weekend of outreach for *The TOUR*, and a few of the rappers were in town for the weekend with some of them camping out at my apartment again. Pastor KNEW the radio station open house was scheduled for that weekend, and he also KNEW that he was expecting me to be a Sunday greeter that morning, but I guess the Lord's servants don't need a day off, so the weekend schedule was made.

My anxiety was controlled but was beating me in the head, as our midnight departure from the radio station the night before had that 7:00 AM morning soundcheck feeling early! I think hell must have frozen over, as well, because it was about twenty degrees outside in

Orlando, Florida, that morning. JESUS, it was cold outside, and my wig wasn't thick enough to keep the breeze out! I generally wear long dresses when I minister, and I was wearing my boots but MY, OH MY, it was cold outside! The cars were classy; the rappers gave God glory; and I attempted to stay warm while videotaping and introducing the next act that was "coming to the stage." Eventually, I noticed that Uncle Bartee was standing in the crowd.

"Did you know your uncle was coming this morning?" I asked JR.

"Naw, Auntie. When he left the radio station last night, he said he was going home. I didn't know he was coming back out to Orlando," he replied.

Now, let me get this straight. This man got off work at the courthouse at 5 PM on Friday, drove over an hour to get from Daytona Beach to Orlando last night, then he returned home and made the same trip again this morning? WOW! This man must REALLY be dedicated to his nephew!

During a DJ music break, I shivered over to him to say hello. I greeted him with a hug, like I do everyone, and I tried to strike up a conversation. He was standing there with a leather trench coat and a leather cap on his bald head; he appeared to be wide awake. I figured it was the cold weather making him look alert because he still didn't seem to be much of a conversationalist with me. I tried to crack jokes – I asked him about the rest of the family ... nothing. *Okay! You can stand there in the parking lot alone for all I care. I tried to show you some fellowship, and you can't even hold a simple conversation?!* I went back to work, dancing, praising, and listening for instructions from the Lord.

Now, my fingers were cold, and we were only halfway into the concert. *I wonder who I can steal some gloves from*, I thought to myself. Just then, JR was preparing to hit the stage. I looked around to be sure his uncle was in place so he didn't miss his nephew's performance, and there he was ... standing alone.

I introduced JR, passed him the microphone, and then headed over to the uncle. His nephew was doing his thang and had the crowd shouting for Christ. Suddenly, I linked my arm around Uncle Bartee's arm. Don't ask me why I did it. Maybe I was trying to warm up to that leather coat of his, but it felt good. He looked at me with a furrowed brow, but he didn't discourage me, so we stood there with arms linked during his nephew's entire set. Throughout the rest of the concert, the same pattern would occur ... I would introduce an act, they would take the microphone, and I would stand alongside Uncle Bartee. Sometimes, I stuck my cold hands in his coat pockets to keep warm, and it felt really good.

From left to right:
"Uncle Bartee", JR, and "Da Queen Bee"

The concert was over, and I was STARVING! I generally fast and pray the day of an outreach event, and I don't snack during our ministry engagement; so, by the time we got off the stage, I needed to find something to eat. This particular weekend, we were scheduled to have a meeting with the rappers, and they wanted to meet before we went to the restaurant. I approached Uncle Bartee and said, "I would like to speak with you after our meeting. Can you please give me a few minutes before you leave?" He said that he would wait, and then we all entered the back room.

I know now what Jesus must have felt like as the disciples argued amongst themselves each night.

"I could have done this song."

"I should have done that prayer," they argued.

"Why didn't we move into the building when the sound went out?"

"Why not this...?" or "Why not that...?" they questioned.

About an hour or so later, I emerged from that room to search for Uncle Bartee, and there he was ... sitting patiently, playing with JR's baby.

According to Bartee

"But I wasn't sitting patiently; I was getting ready to leave!"

When he saw me exit the room, his eyes softened, and this HUGE smile crept across his face. This was the first time I remember seeing his pearly white teeth, and I think he may have even grown a couple of inches taller while I was in that back room.

"What are you going to do now?" he asked.

"I'm hungry! Are you hungry?" I replied.

"I could stand to eat a little something," he said.

And that was that! We were headed to Red Lobster for our FIRST official date!!

After the Deaths, He Enlarged Our Territory

Genesis 1:28, NIV, says: *God blessed them and said to them, "Be fruitful and increase in number."*

At the time I met Bartee, *The TOUR that Angie BEE Presents* had about twelve rappers and a DJ on our roster. On average, there were five or six rappers who attended a concert, and I was always the videographer, photographer, the booking and travel agent, and the MC. That was in February 2013. Now, as I look at our *TOUR* roster in January 2017, I can see how the Lord has allowed Bartee and I to *increase in number* and reach through this ministry:

- There are approximately sixty-two (62) members of *The TOUR that Angie BEE Presents* including several pastors, elders, authors, teachers, and entrepreneurs who are now a part of *The TOUR*, in addition to the original Christian Rappers that started this ministry with me.

- I have been ordained to serve as an evangelist by my pastor, at my new church home in Daytona Beach.

- We now have SIX workshops that travel with *The TOUR* and even minister separately from the original concert event.

- We bring "Movies Under the Stars with Bartee" to communities, as well as Motown game night and fellowship events to churches and senior citizen retirement centers.

- I have written a second book, contributed to a third book, and my company now offers audio book production for other authors. (If you don't have THIS book in the audio format, you are truly missing out on our finest masterpiece.)

- Bartee now leads the *Dads-On-Duty* workshop where the men enter "The Man Cave" to share testimonies and more. (Women are not allowed to enter the Man Cave, so they may be just watching football during those workshops... I don't even know!)

According to Bartee

No, we are not watching sports. We're talking about making the family stronger from a male perspective.

- Bartee and I lead the marriage workshop and retreat entitled *God Me & You*, and he accompanies me to speaking engagements, book signings and appearances. We even bring an annual family retreat weekend that includes a concert, parenting workshops, and FUN!

The generalized anxiety disorder that used to paralyze me is now managed more effectively. During meetings and negotiations, my hubby even says, "Don't stress my wife. You wouldn't like her when she is stressed." (He must think that I am the Incredible Hulk.)

According to Bartee

No, I don't say that. I just say that you can't handle a lot of stress.

But … there have been times when I am lost and darkness is all around me that I hear Bartee's voice bringing me back to home.

Blessings

The house that Bartee rented for five years before he met me was sold to us by the owner in December 2013, just four months after we married. The homeowner LOVES us and our testimony, so she sold the house to us under market and paid all the closing costs. She even added an enclosed back porch onto the house a few months before asking us to buy it from her. Thank you, God!

In January 2016, we held our first marriage retreat; it ended with me driving home a new Volvo SUV. It's almost the exact same color as the convertible Volvo that my hubby was blessed to purchase in December 2014. We're still learning each other, and every now and then, the old me crops up: "Why do I have to submit? Why can't YOU submit?" Then the Lord reminds that we BOTH submit to Him, and He orders our footsteps. Submission leads to blessings! This is why our union and this ministry has been blessed.

Churches and communities book us both to MC and entertain at their events, and it is always SUCH a pleasure to minister alongside my handsome Prince. Sometimes, a church will book him to sing, and then invite me to MC when they realize who we are TOGETHER! This is such a blessing!

Transitions

The dark days hit early in our marriage. Jarvis was THRILLED to hear that we were getting married, and although I was leaving Orlando to move to Daytona Beach, he was praising God for the transition. You see, Jarvis was born and raised in Daytona and had a dream to open a gospel radio station in his hometown. Now that I was moving there, he kept filling me with all these ideas of having me on the Board of Directors and bringing my holy hip hop show to the local airwaves. He even once told me that I should start a morning show and do more "talk radio" rather than hiding in between the music on my show.

Jarvis Smith

Today, I can smile at those memories. Jarvis indeed opened his FM radio station not too long after Bartee and I got married in August 2013; and in April 2015, Jarvis passed away. My friend, Jarvis Smith, left a beautiful and talented widow and two young children. He was only thirty-four years old. My husband handled my grief like a pro and even helped me videotape a memorial DVD of the funeral that I gave to the family. I miss my friend – the one who "saw something in the atmosphere" and who brought gospel music to Daytona Beach.

Now, Back to the Love!

Bartee had proposed to me on May 8, 2013, which was my birthday. He had a restaurant dinner party for me in Orlando that my daughters and my friends attended. We had talked about marriage but he wanted us to wait a bit before we got married as he said it was just too soon to get married. We had only met in February, just a few months earlier; however, whenever we would be out shopping and I would not be instantly in his line of vision, he would loudly state, "Where is my wife?"

Upon hearing his voice, I would jump back by his side and say, "I don't know where your wife is, but I'm here for ya!"

Dinner was ending, and I had opened all my birthday gifts. There was a card from Bartee but no ring-in-the-box. I knew that he HAD a ring because he had shown it to me. He said that he was thinking about buying a ring from his co-worker, and he wanted to know if I liked it. I told him that I did, and then it went back in his pocket. That was about a month earlier, and he hadn't mentioned it again.

It was just about time for hugs and goodbyes as I was gathering up all my gift bags when Bartee drops his napkin on the floor of the restaurant. When he bent down to pick it up, I went into mother-mode. "Here, I have a napkin for you! Just leave that one on the floor," and I reached out to hand him my napkin. It was then that I realized that he was on one knee, and there was a ring box in his hand. With a tear in his eye, "Uncle Bartee" proposed to me, "Da Queen Bee," Angie BEE.

He proposed on May 8th and then … we were both booked solid until August 9th. When I say booked, we were BOOKED! If *The TOUR* wasn't doing outreach one weekend, Bartee was doing a concert another weekend. I had a book signing or two, and then, he provided entertainment at a hotel on the beachside. The only time I knew we had a week off was the week I was taking him to Detroit to meet my family. We were bringing the *Moms-n-Ministry* workshop to a church in Ocala,

Florida, on August 9th, and then we were leaving on August 14th to meet the kinfolk.

I prayed to God, asking Him to hold my hand and lead me on HIS path during that summer, as the radio show had become syndicated to air on roughly five or six additional stations. I was continuing to lose weight from the gastric bypass surgery I'd had in February 2010, and Bartee was starting to eat smaller portions, too! We kept trying to plan a wedding to include our families, and we discussed something on the beach or at a community center. Bartee kept introducing me to folks in Daytona Beach, and I started going to counseling to deal with symptoms of a new diagnosis: PTSD.

Jarvis had introduced us to Bishop Ann, and we were headed to her church in Ocala for a weekend of outreach when my fiancé looked at me and said, "We should get married before we head to Detroit. It just wouldn't be right to meet them and we aren't married."

So that's what we did!

On Friday, August 9, 2013, I headed to the courthouse with my youngest daughter and my friend Reverend Dawn Martin. I met Bartee during his lunch break, and we exchanged vows in the same courthouse chapel where we first met.

Reverend Dawn was in town to participate in the *Moms-n-Ministry* workshop that weekend. When I called her and told her that we were making a stop at the courthouse before heading to the workshop, she just about shouted for joy! As an experienced event planner and a travel agent by trade, she began to ask me all sorts of logistical questions. I told her that we were following God's schedule, and I just knew to arrive at the courthouse at 1 PM, which was Bartee's lunch break.

On Thursday night, Bartee and I were packing and preparing for not only the weekend workshop, but for our wedding as well, and Rev. Dawn was with us! Now, three years later these are the thoughts that Rev. Dawn shared with me about the night:

I remember that day like it was yesterday. Angie looked so pretty and HAPPY for the first time since I had met her. I recall that evening before (the wedding) being at the house and Bartee saying, "It's time to go shave," and they both proceeded into the bedroom/bathroom. Moments later, they both came out with shaving cream on both of their heads! I laughed at first, but then I looked a little closer at what GOD had done for my friend. After battling years of Alopecia, she had finally found someone that would truly LOVE her for ALL that she is and ALL that she looks like inside and out.

I knew then HE WAS HER BOAZ!! AMEN

Do you remember earlier in the story when I told you about all those dresses I had been accumulating? Well, one of those was a lovely, full-length white gown with spaghetti straps that just-so-happened to be on clearance sale. I thought it would be perfect, but I really wanted to surprise Bartee with something special, so I borrowed a veil from my best friend Gwendolyn. She was still asking me if I had lost my mind because I like tall, thin, yellow men with wavy hair; and this was a short, round, chocolate man that was bald. LOL! It takes a true friend to make you pray over something, and Gwendolyn is a true friend.

I drove to the courthouse, went through the metal detectors, and allowed Dawn and my daughter to enter the room to be sure that Bartee was there. As I stood in the hallway waiting to enter the chapel, I remember thinking, *I hope we aren't late arriving at Bishop Ann's church*. We were scheduled for the meet and greet later that evening, and the workshop was scheduled for the next morning.

As I planned out our trip earlier that week, I had called and talked to her, "Bishop Ann? We will be dressed a little strangely when we arrive at your church. We are getting married at 1 PM on Friday, and we won't have time to change clothes before we arrive."

Bishop Ann couldn't believe that we were still planning to minister on our honeymoon weekend, but God was ordering our footsteps, and she gave Him praise for our obedience.

Back at the Courthouse

"Dearly Beloved ..." those words began again as I stood next to Uncle Bartee. His eye glistened, and he exchanged his vows with a wondrous gaze in his eyes. When I arrived by his side upon entering the chapel, he looked at me and gently fingered by veil. "You look like a bride!" he whispered in amazement. The day that we wed was August 9, 2013.

"I'm not A bride, I am YOUR bride," I responded.

His boss was there to witness our vows, and even my friend Ayana from Orlando traveled to DeLand to share our special moment with us.

According to Bartee

Well, the way I seen it, I wasn't really ready to get married again, and God had put this smart and lovely lady in my path. I had some choices to make in order to receive His blessing. So, I made the choice of receiving His blessings, and I decided to marry this smart and lovely lady. Sometimes, people can pass up blessings because you make the wrong choice. I'm just an average guy, no more than any other man. I just try to live-and-let-live and keep God first ... and thank Him every day for my life, health and strength, and many blessings that He bestowed upon me.

LIFE IS GOOD!

She Was There!

There is a young woman in my life that attended our very first *Moms-n-Ministry* workshop back in January 2013. She is a radio announcer, and her stage name is Yanni Ayana. Her pastor encouraged her to attend the workshop, even though she is not a mother. Afterwards, we struck up a conversation, our fellowship began, and I even featured her ministry segments on my daily radio show. She is a jewel in my life, and she traveled from Orlando, Florida, to DeLand to attend our wedding. This is what she said:

God bless Bartee & Angie Bee!

As I entered the marriage ceremony, I saw the love (between) two wonderful people, who beamed with gratitude unto the Lord for another chance of love and eternal covenant. Light, love, & joy radiated from everyone, especially the bride & groom!

To God be the Glory for this amazing couple! Bartee and Angie Bee have a powerful, impactful, beautiful ministry of love, evangelism, and giving.

After having lunch at Bartee's favorite lunchtime spot and showing off his new bride, Rev. Dawn, Bartee, and I headed to Ocala to minister alongside Bishop Ann. She was sitting in her car in the parking lot when we arrived; and although I had not met her face-to-face prior to that moment, I instantly knew who she was. My new spiritual mother was filled with joy at our arrival and promptly paraded us around in our wedding attire to meet everyone. The meet and greet was splendid, and the hotel room was extra special. The *Moms-n-Ministry* workshop the next morning was TRULY a blessing … and then, there was Sunday morning service.

Now, Bartee and I may have exchanged vows at the courthouse that Friday, but Bishop Ann truly married us during Sunday morning service. Unexpectedly, she shared with the congregation how Jarvis had connected us and how I came highly recommended as a minister of the Gospel. She spoke about how we arrived on Friday night in our wedding garments and brought the meet and greet AND moms' workshop to the church. She shared with the congregation that *The TOUR* does not charge an honorarium and that we brought door prizes of glorious baskets to share with the mothers. Then, she called my husband and me up to the front for prayer.

Bishop Ann PRAYED over us! She broke soul ties and restored broken hearts. She prophesied that MANY ministries would be birthed through our union, and she touched my belly to plant that seed. Bartee stood by my side as I felt a wave of love and anointing enter me, and my head was spinning as tears of joy streamed down my face. At that moment, I felt complete submission to this "Boaz" who stood by my side. I felt a release from the guilt of keeping my daughters in a domestically violent home with my second husband, and I no longer felt the shame of my first husband's abandonment. I felt brand new! I felt like I was being immersed in a baptismal pool of refreshment, and when I opened my eyes, Bartee was standing there.

A month later, Bishop Ann invited us to be her guests during her annual birthday party. She encouraged us to dance, and she bragged about how we were her son and daughter, and how we ministered at her church before leaving for our wedding bed. It was a beautiful affair, and I was so excited to be with my spiritual mom again. She had accepted me as hers, and she promised to introduce us to her other church leaders in affiliation. In the spring of 2014, I returned to Ocala where I served as MC of her weekend women's retreat, and Bartee served as videographer. I loved my life; I loved this ministry; I loved my husband; and Bishop Ann loved us.

Then, in January 2015, we found ourselves traveling to Tampa to videotape Bishop Ann's funeral. She'd had to reconcile a church that was about to split. She was used to ushering in a spirit of restoration and reconciliation to the families and the church; she was simply doing what she loved to do! The next day she was rushed to the hospital where her family gathered to say their goodbyes. Our beloved Bishop Ann transitioned on Christmas Eve, December 24, 2014; Christmas was her favorite time of the year.

Now, we were traveling to say our goodbyes. My friend Gwendolyn accompanied Bartee and me to the funeral, and one of the praise dancers from *The TOUR* joined in the service. Tahara looked regal as she carried the flag and danced with the others, but I was numb ... I really was. You see, as long as Bishop Ann was my spiritual mother, I felt that *The TOUR* could grow and have a covering. Now, she was gone. I remember feeling this way when my own mother died in November 1999. *Who was going to help me raise my daughters? Who was going to be sure that I didn't poison them or do something wrong?* My earthly mother left when my kids were young, and now my spiritual mother was gone, and this ministry was young! I was so empty inside.

Bishop Ann Evans speaking at the Moms-n-Ministry Workshop, August 10, 2013

A Word from God

Our good friend and *TOUR* member, Prophetess Veronica, met us for lunch after the funeral service concluded just to give us a word from the Lord. She said that *The TOUR* would grow to such a size that some of us would minister in one area, while Angie BEE & Bartee would minister in another area. This word has already begun to unfold. She told me to come out from behind the "veil" of the background and step into the foreground with Bartee by my side. I'm doing that. She said that my temple would continue to be restored, and I see that happening. She also said that Bartee would record an original CD. Don't worry ... it's coming (Lord willing)!

It's January 2017. I realize that we have been married now for as long as some other people have been dating! God has been with us every step of the way. Bartee has a book inside of him, and he wants to write it soon. In the meantime, I'll let him chime in on my book(s)! God has still been faithful in providing the finances for our door prizes, our travel, and our hotel stays when *The TOUR* goes out to minister; and now, Bartee is our official DJ. All that speaker equipment that he had been collecting in the garage is now dedicated to *The TOUR*. THANK YOU, GOD!

In the fall of 2017, we will introduce our singles workshop and retreat, and God will send us the anointed ministry leaders who will participate. I see a beachside event with food on the grill, marshmallows roasting after sunset, and the Love of the Lord coming through the ocean waves! Now, a few MORE intimate details of our courtship are not shared in this book; you will only hear THOSE stories during the workshops (so you HAVE to attend). I will share a couple if tidbits with you now, just to entice you to attend:

- How did I reveal to Bartee that I am a completely bald woman?

- How did submission to Bartee teach me to receive love from others?

- How does 2 Corinthians 9:8 describe our love?

- How does 1 Corinthians 7:4 lead to submission?

I thank the Lord for being there, ordering our footsteps as we walked this path of love and fellowship ... and, I thank our Father for blinding our eyes towards each other. I know that Bartee was not my type, and I was not his ... but God knew what we needed. *In the Beginning: There was God, Me & You*, and I pray that it will be that way until the end.

BEE Blessed

Photo and Makeup by The Anointed Lesley Reed
A member of ***The TOUR that Angie BEE Presents***

ANGIE BEE Presents... The Tour

Invite **The TOUR that Angie BEE Presents** to your conference, workshop, or gathering!

Search for #TheTOURthatAngieBEEpresents and LIKE us on Facebook at
www.Facebook.com/TheTOURthatAngieBEEpresents

Come LIKE our workshop pages at

www.Facebook.com/MomsNministry

www.Facebook.com/AngieBEEpresentsDadsOnDuty

www.Facebook.com/CanYouHearMeImHurting

www.Facebook.com/GodMeAndYou

We invite you to come and LIKE our pages!

www.Facebook.com/AngieBEEandBarteeProductions

www.Facebook.com/DaQueenBeeEvangelistAngieBEE

Follow us on Twitter at
@TheTOURthatAngieBEEpresents

Search for Bartee The Rage of the Stage on
www.GigSalad.com

www.DaQueenBee.com

We hope to hear from you soon!

Evangelist Angie BEE serves as a board member of this non-profit 501(c) (3) organization. We invite you to support

Sword of the Spirit Ministries, Florida, Inc.